CRAFTING FOR CHANGE

CREATE JOY with Crafts

by Ruthie Van Oosbree

raintree
a Capstone company — publishers for children

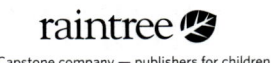

Raintree is an imprint of Capstone Global Library Limited, a company incorporated in England and Wales having its registered office at 264 Banbury Road, Oxford, OX2 7DY –
Registered company number: 6695582

www.raintree.co.uk
myorders@raintree.co.uk

Text © Capstone Global Library Limited 2025
The moral rights of the proprietor have been asserted.

All rights reserved. No part of this publication may be reproduced in any form or by any means (including photocopying or storing it in any medium by electronic means and whether or not transiently or incidentally to some other use of this publication) without the written permission of the copyright owner, except in accordance with the provisions of the Copyright, Designs and Patents Act 1988 or under the terms of a licence issued by the Copyright Licensing Agency, 5th Floor, Shackleton House, 4 Battle Bridge Lane, London, SE1 2HX (www.cla.co.uk). Applications for the copyright owner's written permission should be addressed to the publisher.

Edited by Jessica Rusick
Designed by Sarah DeYoung and Denise Hamernik
Media Research by Rebekah Hubstenberger
Projects by Ruthie Van Oosbree and Chelsey Luciow
Originated by Capstone Global Library Ltd

ISBN 978 1 3982 5561 6

British Library Cataloguing in Publication Data
A full catalogue record for this book is available from the British Library.

Acknowledgements
We would like to thank the following for permission to reproduce photographs: Adobe Stock: Asier, 4; Mighty Media, Inc.: project photos. Design Elements: iStockphoto: Bakai, Dmytro Synelnychenko, mightyisland; Mighty Media, Inc.

Every effort has been made to contact copyright holders of material reproduced in this book. Any omissions will be rectified in subsequent printings if notice is given to the publisher.

All the internet addresses (URLs) given in this book were valid at the time of going to press. However, due to the dynamic nature of the internet, some addresses may have changed, or sites may have changed or ceased to exist since publication. While the author and publisher regret any inconvenience this may cause readers, no responsibility for any such changes can be accepted by either the author or the publisher.

Contents

Crafting for joy 4
Cheerful chimes 6
Pocket hug. 8
Sweetie jar 10
Super stones. 12
Window warmers 14
Clown jar 16
Pencil poppers 18
Brighter day box 20
Stitch a smile 24
Friendly fairy garden. 28
   Find out more 32
   About the author 32

Crafting for joy

Do you want to change the world? Start crafting! Whether you're hoping to brighten a neighbour's day, warm a family member's heart or make a friend laugh, the crafts in this book are bound to bring a smile to someone's face. Plus, these projects are great fun to make and share. You'll love creating joy in your community!

What is craftivism?

Craftivism is the act of using crafts to make a change in your community. It is short for "craft activism". People make crafts to protest against issues, draw attention to causes and help build a better world. Craftivism can be used for social justice, environmentalism, peace, political change and more. Use the projects in this book to become a craftivist for a more joyful world!

BASIC SUPPLIES

beads * coloured paper * decorative paper * felt * glue stick * hot glue gun * paint and paintbrushes * pencil and paper * ruler * scissors * string * yarn

Craftivism tips

1. **Prepare.** Collect all your materials and supplies and read through the instructions carefully before starting a project. Cover your workspace with newspaper or another covering to protect it from spills.

2. **Ask first.** Before you start crafting, ask permission to use any supplies you find.

3. **Stay safe.** Ask an adult for help using hot or sharp tools or hammers. Place scrap wood under items before hammering holes into them to protect surfaces.

4. **Clean up.** Tidy up after you've finished crafting. Put supplies back where you found them and clean up your workspace.

5. **Keep it temporary.** Craftivism projects shouldn't permanently alter public spaces. Respect these spaces and be considerate of other people.

Cheerful chimes

This wind chime doesn't just create soothing nature sounds – its colourful design also brings cheer to anyone who catches a glimpse!

Supplies
- 6 medium-sized sticks
- paint and paintbrushes
- large plastic storage lid
- hammer and nail
- string
- ruler
- scissors

1. Paint the sticks in bright colours. Let them dry. If you like, paint patterns onto the sticks and let them dry again.

2. Use the hammer and nail to make six holes in the centre of the storage lid. Poke the nail through each hole and wiggle it around to make the holes larger.

3. Cut six lengths of string about 50 cm long.

4. Wrap one end of a length of string around the end of a stick. Tie a knot to secure. Try to tie the string underneath any little bits sticking out of the stick. This will help to keep the string secured.

5. Thread the string up through a hole in the storage lid. Choose how low you want the stick to hang from the lid.

6. Knot the string five to ten times on top of the lid. Cut off excess string.

7. Repeat steps 4 to 6 with the remaining sticks.

8. Balance your wind chime on a tree branch, porch beam or fence outside where it will make calming music on a breezy day!

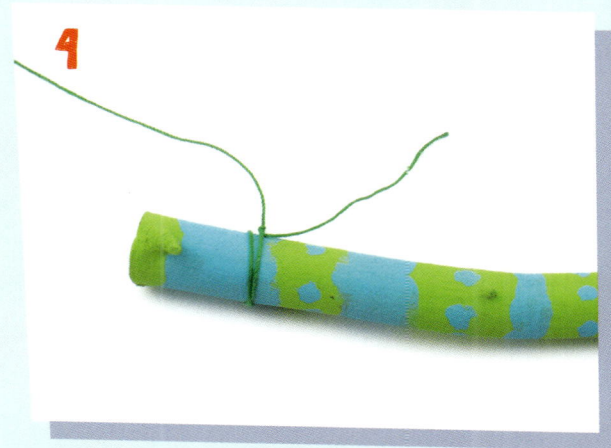

CRAFTIVISM TIP

Make several wind chimes! Then ask your town council if you can hang the chimes at local parks.

Pocket hug

Is your friend feeling down? Does your family member live far away? Give them hugs even when you're not next to them by gifting them an adorable pocket hug to carry!

Supplies
- pencil and paper
- felt in assorted colours
- fabric marker pens
- scissors
- embroidery thread in assorted colours
- sewing needle
- fabric glue
- newspaper

1. Use pencil and paper to sketch a design for an animal peeking out of a pocket. Include a pocket shape, face and paws.

2. Fold the felt in half to create two layers. Draw the elements of the design on the felt using fabric marker pen. Then cut the designs out.

3. Stack the pocket cut-outs on top of each other so that the parts marked by fabric marker pen are on the inside. Use the needle and embroidery thread to sew around the bottom and sides of the pocket.

4. Repeat step 3 to sew the top and sides of the animal's face.

5. Cut any facial features for the animal out of felt. These could include a nose, ears and spots. Glue the felt cut-outs to the face. Let the glue dry.

6. Use embroidery thread to add other facial features, such as a mouth, to the animal's face.

7. Shred the newspaper. Stuff the shreds into the openings of the face and pocket. Leave a small amount unstuffed for sewing.

8. Place the bottom of the animal's face into the unstuffed portion of the pocket. Sew across the top of the pocket, stitching through the bottom of the animal's face as you go.

9. Glue the paws to the front of the pocket. Let the glue dry.

10. Give your pocket hug to a pal so they have a warm, fuzzy friend!

Sweetie Jar

Sweets are a surprise that will make just about anybody's day! Share the joy in a fun gumball machine–style jar that's bound to delight.

Supplies

- clay flowerpot and drip tray about 13 to 15 centimetres across at widest sections
- small wooden spool or round wooden bead
- paint and paintbrush
- round glass or plastic rose bowl 15 cm across at widest point
- hot glue gun
- black paper
- medium-sized metal washer
- metal bit, such as a toggle bolt or wing nut
- scissors
- glue stick
- small, wrapped sweets

1. Paint the flowerpot, drip tray and wooden spool or bead in the colour of your choice.

2. Turn the flowerpot upside down. Use the hot glue gun to glue the bottom of the bowl to the bottom of the flowerpot.

3. Hot glue the wooden spool or bead to the bottom of the drip pan.

4. Cut an arched shape out of black paper. Use the glue stick to attach it above the rim of the flowerpot.

5. Hot glue the washer onto the flowerpot beneath the bowl. Then hot glue the toggle bolt or wing nut onto the bottom of the washer.

6. Fill the bowl with sweets and place the drip tray on top. Set your "gumball machine" up to share the sweets out!

Keep crafting!

If you plan to take your sweetie jar to school or an event, make it with a plastic flowerpot and bowl so it's more durable.

CRAFTIVISM TIP

Share your sweetie jar with librarians, teachers or other people in your community who deserve recognition!

Super stones

Brighten neighbours' days by placing these bold and beautiful decorative stones along pavements!

Supplies
* smooth, flat stones
* paint (white, assorted colours) and paintbrushes
* paint pens
* permanent marker pen

1. Paint the tops of the stones white. Let the paint dry.

2. Paint designs on the stones in assorted colours. Let the paint dry.

3. Use the paint pens to write positive messages on the stones. Let the paint dry.

4. Use permanent marker pen to trace around or otherwise highlight the messages. Then line the stones along a pavement for passers-by to see!

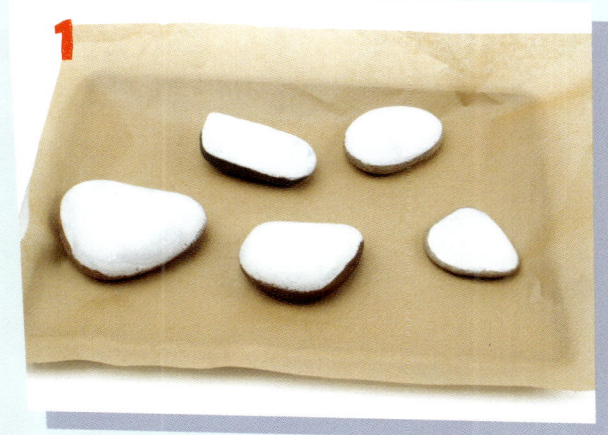

Keep crafting!

If you have many small stones, try creating a design that uses all of them! Paint each one a solid colour. Then arrange them in a design. Black and yellow stones could be arranged into a smiling sun. Brown and green stones could be arranged into a tree!

CRAFTIVISM TIP

You can also place the stones in parks or other public spaces for others to enjoy. But don't leave the rocks at national parks or on private property.

Window warmers

This beautiful window display is a simple but effective way to cheer up your neighbours' day!

Supplies
* paper and pencil
* scissors
* felt in assorted colours
* ruler
* yarn or string
* hot glue gun

1. Fold a piece of paper in half. Draw half a heart along the folded edge. Cut it out and unfold it. This heart will work as a stencil for cutting out hearts from felt.

2. Decide how many garlands you will make. You will need 18 to 20 felt hearts per garland. Use the stencil to cut out felt hearts, making two of each colour.

3. Cut a piece of yarn or string about 1 metre long. Tie a loop in one end. This will be the top of the garland.

4. Arrange the hearts in same-colour pairs next to the string in the order you want them to hang.

5. Add a strip of hot glue down the centre of the first heart. Place the yarn or string onto the glue. Glue the second piece of each heart on top of the first piece.

6. Repeat step 5 with the remaining hearts, gluing each one 5 cm further down the string.

7. Repeat steps 3 to 6 to create additional garlands. Hang them in a window so that people walking past can see them!

CRAFTIVISM TIP

Create garlands that spell out positive messages, such as "be kind" or "you are strong".

Clown jar

People often say that laughter is the best medicine. Treat friends to a laugh with a clown-themed jar filled with jokes!

Supplies
- large, clean glass jar
- scissors
- white tissue paper
- small bowl
- white PVA glue
- sponge brush
- paper in assorted colours
- hole punch
- hot glue gun
- pom-poms
- black felt-tip pen or marker pen
- internet or library access

1. Cut a piece of tissue paper long enough to wrap around the jar.

2. Pour several tablespoons of PVA glue into the small bowl. Brush glue onto the jar. Then wrap the tissue paper around the jar and smooth it down. Trim off excess tissue paper and brush glue over any spots that aren't sticking down. Let the glue dry.

3. While the jar dries, use the hole punch to cut circles or other shapes out of the coloured paper.

4. Lightly brush glue over a small section of the jar. Place cut-out shapes onto this area and brush glue over them. Repeat this process until the jar is covered in shapes. Let the jar dry.

5. Hot glue pom-poms around the top of the jar.

6. Cut 15 to 20 strips of paper about 5 cm × 13 cm. Fold the strips in half.

7. Research jokes online or at the library. Write the question part of each joke on the front of a paper strip in black felt-tip pen or marker pen. Write the answer inside the paper.

8. Put the folded jokes in the jar. Get friends to draw jokes out of the jar when they need a laugh!

CRAFTIVISM TIP

Encourage your community to get involved in the project. Ask friends and family if they would like to add jokes to your jar!

Pencil Poppers

These pencil windmills are a pretty — and pretty fun — way to bring joy to others!

Supplies
- 2-sided decorative paper
- ruler
- pencil
- scissors
- sewing pins
- pliers
- pencils with erasers

1. Cut a square 10 cm × 10 cm out of decorative paper.

2. Use the ruler and pencil to mark the centre of the square, 5 cm in from any corner.

3. Cut from each corner towards the centre, stopping about 1.5 cm before you reach the centre. This creates four triangles pointing towards the centre.

4. Tuck the bottom-right corner of each triangle up to the centre. Hold the corners in place.

5. Stick a sewing pin through the centre so it goes through all four corners and the main square.

6. Use pliers to bend the pointed end of the pin downwards at a 90 degree angle.

7. Repeat steps 1–6 to create more windmills. Their pins can be stuck into pencil erasers to make joyful pencil toppers!

4

6

CRAFTIVISM TIP

Ask a local care home if you can share the windmills with residents!

Brighter day box

Help raise the spirits of a child in hospital by sending a box filled with fun things to do!

Supplies

- toys, games, books and other items to donate to a child
- plastic storage box
- paper in bright colours and patterns
- scissors
- pencil
- jar lid or glass for tracing
- glue stick
- tape
- white paper
- felt-tip pens

1. Collect items to donate. Products should be new and still in their original packaging. Make sure you research guidelines for accepted items of the organization or hospital you're donating to.

2. Fold or cut a piece of coloured paper to fit in the centre of the plastic box's lid.

3. Cut wedges of coloured paper to make sun rays.

CRAFTIVISM TIP

Donations can be posted directly to hospitals or dropped off in person. Call the hospital or look online to see which method is preferred.

Project continues on the next page.

4. Use the jar lid or glass to trace a circle onto coloured paper. Cut it out. Use this circle to cut a slightly larger circle out of a different colour. Glue the smaller circle onto the larger circle. This is the sun.

5. Arrange the rays on the box lid paper, allowing some of the background colour to show. Glue the rays in place. Then glue the sun on top of the rays.

6. Trim off any excess paper from the rays. Save these scraps for later in the project! Tape the sun paper onto the box lid.

7. Now make a card. Lightly draw a circle on a white piece of paper. Cut the scraps from step 6 into triangles of different sizes. Arrange them in a mosaic inside the circle. Glue the triangles in place and cut the circle out.

8. Draw a cloud shape on a piece of white paper and cut it out. Glue the cloud onto a piece of coloured paper and cut around it, creating a border.

9. Glue the cloud onto the circle mosaic. Use felt-tip pens to draw dots in the gaps between pieces of the mosaic. Write a positive message in the cloud.

10. Fold a piece of coloured paper in half to make a card. Glue the mosaic circle and cloud onto the front of the card.

11. Glue white paper inside the card. Use felt-tip pens to write a positive note on the paper. Deliver your card with your box of goodies to brighten someone's day!

CRAFTIVISM TIP

Try to avoid using phrases such as "Get well soon" or "Feel better" in your card. Not all children in the hospital will have conditions they can recover from. Some hospitals and organizations have recommended messages online.

Stitch a smile

If you're looking for a joyful decoration to brighten your home, look no further than this sweet design with a charming message!

Supplies

- paper and pencil
- fabric, such as embroidery fabric or a tea towel
- washable marker pen or water-soluble fabric marker pen
- 15-cm embroidery hoop
- yarn in yellow, black and white
- yarn needle that can fit through bead openings
- beads
- string
- letter beads

1. Draw a simple bee with paper and pencil. Give the bee stripes, wings and antennae.

2. Use washable marker or fabric marker to draw the bee design on fabric. You may be able to trace the design if your fabric is transparent enough! Secure the fabric in the embroidery hoop with the design above the centre.

3. Cut a piece of yellow yarn about 6 cm long and thread it through the yarn needle. Tie a knot on the other end.

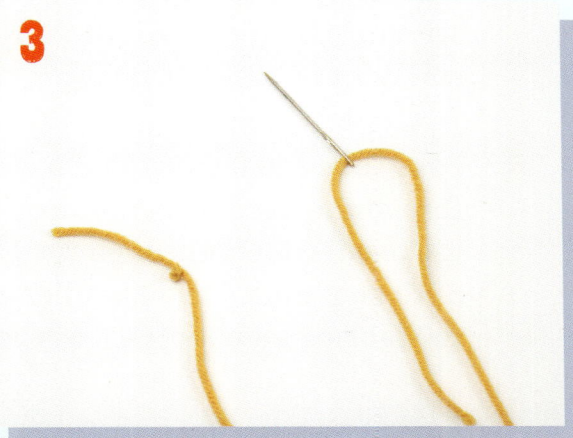

Project continues on the next page.

4. Push the needle up through the fabric from the back. Start at the top left of the first yellow stripe. Stitch across the bee's body to fill in this first stripe. Then fill in the remaining yellow stripes. When finished, tie a knot behind the fabric and cut off excess yarn.

5. Repeat steps 3 and 4 with black yarn to fill in the black stripes.

6. Repeat step 3 with white yarn. Fill in the wings, stitching up and down across each one. Tie a knot behind the fabric and cut off excess yarn.

7. Thread the needle with 30 cm black yarn and tie a knot in the other end. Push the needle up through the fabric near the bee's head. Make short stitches back towards the end of the antenna. Continue stitching in this way until only a small bit of antenna is left.

8. Poke the needle through a bead and thread the bead onto the yarn. Push the needle down through the end of the antenna. Tie a knot behind the fabric and cut off excess yarn.

9. Repeat steps 7 and 8 to stitch the other antenna.

10. Cut a piece of string 30 cm to 60 cm long. Thread it through the needle and tie a knot on the other end. Push the needle up through the fabric under the left side of the bee. Pull the string tight.

11. Poke the needle through the letter beads to spell out "Bee Happy".

12. Push the needle down through the fabric under the bee's right side and pull tightly. Knot the string in the back and cut off any excess. Display your joyful design in a place where it will make you and your family smile!

Keep crafting!

Embroider other materials so you can bring your bee design with you! Stitch your bee onto a tote bag. Think of ways to change the design to suit your needs. For example, you could embroider letters onto a T-shirt instead of using beads!

Friendly fairy garden

A little magic goes a long way! This happy fairy home will warm the hearts of passers-by as they imagine the friendly fairies living there.

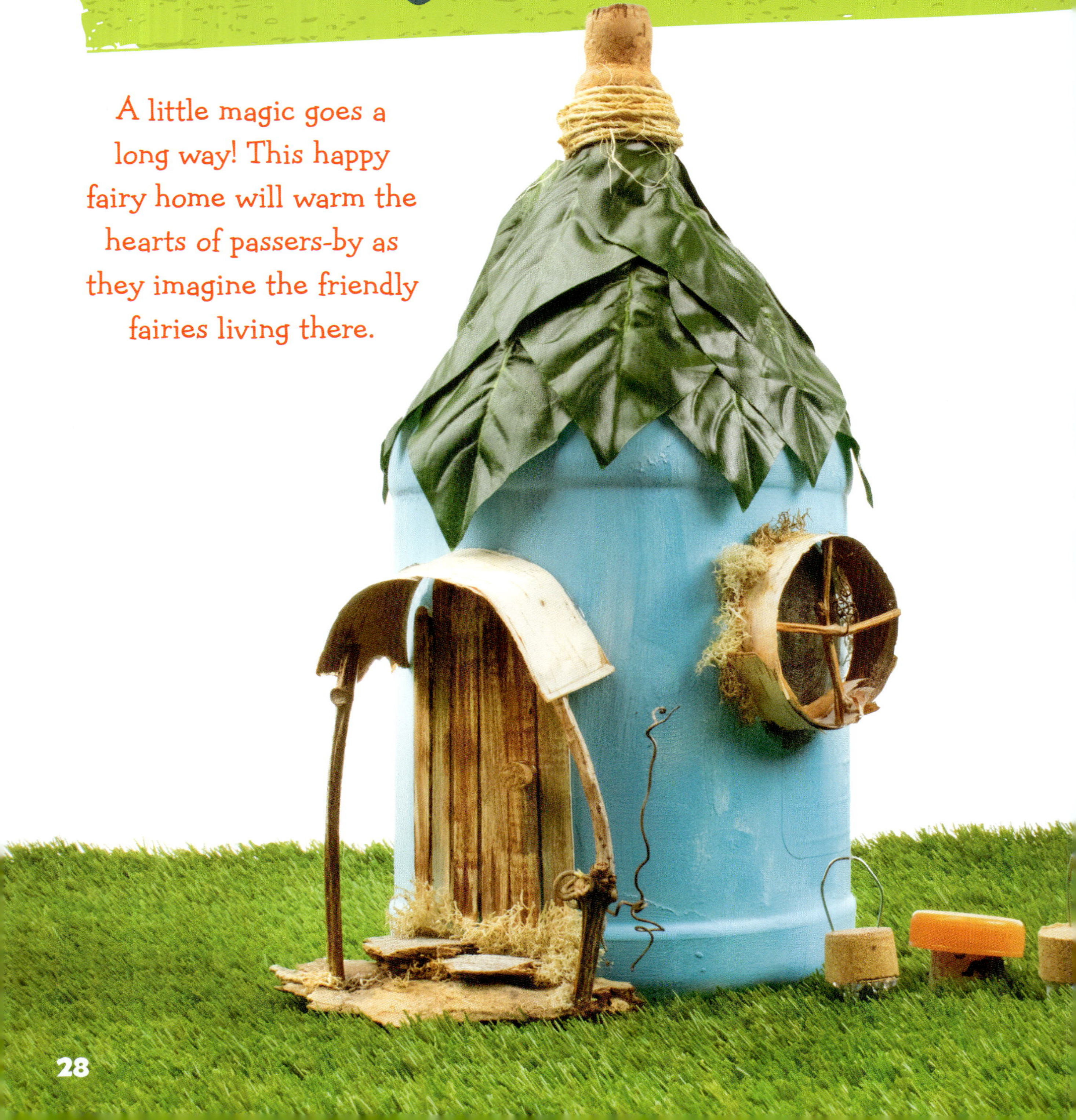

Supplies

- large recycled bottle
- paint and paintbrushes
- corks
- bottle cap
- hot glue gun
- scissors
- straight pin
- paper clips
- wire cutters
- pushpins
- craft sticks
- fake leaves
- twine
- PVA glue
- natural materials, such as twigs, dried vines, moss, birch bark and pebbles

1. Paint the bottle white. Let it dry. Then paint over this base layer in a colour of your choice. Let it dry. This will be the fairy house.

2. While the paint dries, make the table and chairs. For the table, use the hot glue gun to glue a cork to the inside of the bottle cap. Paint the bottle cap if desired.

3. For the chairs, cut a cork into three equal sections with scissors. Discard one piece. Use the straight pin to poke two holes in the remaining pieces of cork. The holes should be across from each other on top of the cork pieces.

Project continues on the next page.

4. Use wire cutters to cut a paper clip and bend it into the shape of a chair-back. Push it into the holes in the cork pieces. Push four pushpins into the bottom of each cork piece for chair legs.

5. Continue crafting the fairy house. Arrange several craft sticks side by side so they are about the size and shape of a door for the house. Trim the bottoms of the craft sticks in a straight line.

6. Hot glue the craft sticks onto the house, starting with the middle, tallest sticks. Paint the door if desired.

7. Glue fake leaves onto the bottle where it begins to narrow. This will be the house's roof. Start with a single bottom row. Then continue up the roof in rows, covering gaps between leaves as you go.

8. Glue a large cork to the top of the house for a chimney. Apply PVA glue to the lower half of the cork. Wrap twine around the cork and hold it in place briefly until it begins to set on its own.

9. Use natural materials to decorate the rest of the house. Add an overhang to the door, front steps, a twig or vine window, and anything else you'd like!

10. Put the fairy house outside. Arrange the table and chairs in front of it. Display the house somewhere your neighbours will see it!

CRAFTIVISM TIP

Organize a community art project by inviting friends and neighbours to make their own fairy homes. Use the homes to make a neighbourhood fairy garden!

Find out more

Books

Eco Craft Book: Don't Throw It Away, Recreate & Play, Laura Minter and Tia Williams (GMC Publications, 2021)

Mini Gifts that Surprise and Delight (Mini Makers), Lauren Kukla (Raintree, 2024)

Rebel Crafts: 15 Craftivism Projects to Change the World, Hester Van Overbeek (Welbeck, 2021)

Websites

www.goodhousekeeping.com/home/craft-ideas/g20967550/summer-crafts/
Check out this website for lots of different craft ideas for you to try.

www.bbc.co.uk/cbbc/curations/bp-arts-and-crafts-collection
Love crafting? Head for the CBBC Blue Peter arts and crafts collection.

About the author

Ruthie Van Oosbree is a writer and editor who loves making crafts. She is passionate about social justice, animal welfare and the environment. She lives with her husband and three adorable cats.